KILLER ANIMALS

GREAT WHITE SHARKS

ON THE HUNT

by Janet Riehecky

Reading Consultant:
Barbara J. Fox
Reading Specialist
North Carolina State University

Content Consultant:
Deborah Nuzzolo
Education Manager
SeaWorld
San Diego, California

Mankato, Minnesota

Blazers is published by Capstone Press,
151 Good Counsel Drive, P.O. Box 669, Mankato, Minnesota 56002.
www.capstonepress.com

Library of Congress Cataloging-in-Publication Data
Riehecky, Janet, 1953–
   Great white sharks: on the hunt/by Janet Riehecky.
   p. cm. — (Blazers. Killer animals)
   Includes bibliographical references and index.
   Summary: "Describes great white sharks, their physical features, how they hunt and kill, and
their role in the ecosystem" — Provided by publisher.
   ISBN-13: 978-1-4296-2315-5 (hardcover)
   ISBN-10: 1-4296-2315-2 (hardcover)
   1. White shark — Juvenile literature. I. Title.
QL638.95.L3R54 2009
597.3'3 — dc22
                                                   2008029835

Editorial Credits

Abby Czeskleba, editor; Kyle Grenz, designer; Wanda Winch, photo researcher

Photo Credits

Art Life Images/Stuart Westmorland, 10–11
Getty Images Inc./AFP/Rodger Bosch, 26–27
marinethemes.com/Andy Murch, 4–5; Kelvin Aitken, 13, 20–21; Mark Conlin, 28–29
Peter Arnold/Biosphoto/J.-L. Klein & M.-L. Hubert, 15; F. Vnoucek, 7; Klaus Jost, cover
SeaPics.com/Amos Nachoum, 22–23; C & M Fallows, 8–9, 16–17, 18–19;
   V & W/Kike Calvo, 25

1 2 3 4 5 6 14 13 12 11 10 09

TABLE OF CONTENTS

SHARK ATTACK

A great white shark quietly swims through the water. It watches a seal swim nearby. Suddenly, the shark rushes toward the seal.

KILLER FACT

Great whites can speed through the water at more than 20 miles (32 kilometers) per hour.

The shark tears off a piece of meat. It **seizes** the seal in its mouth. Dinner is served.

seize – to take something by force

KILLER FACT

A great white can eat a 400-pound
(181-kilogram) seal in about 10 bites.

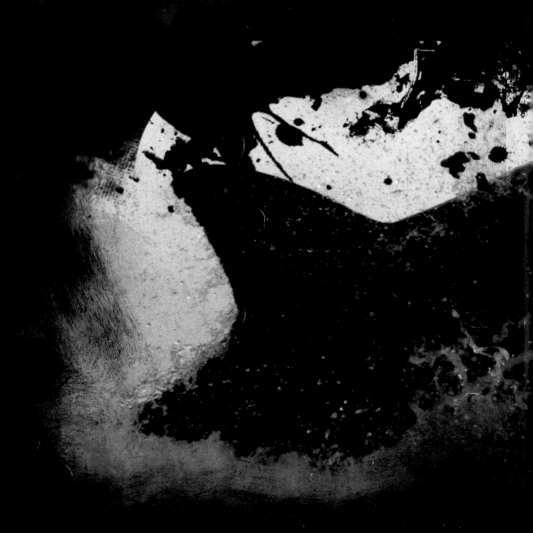

TOOLS OF THE TRADE

Great white sharks are **carnivores**. They are the world's largest meat-eating fish. They weigh more than 4,000 pounds (1,814 kilograms). Great whites can grow up to 15 feet (4.6 meters) long.

carnivore – an animal that eats only meat

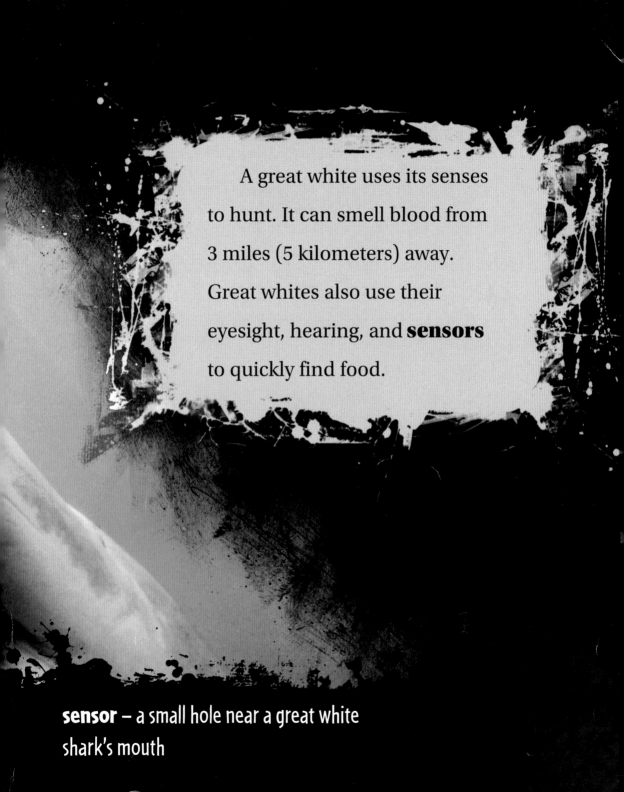

A great white uses its senses to hunt. It can smell blood from 3 miles (5 kilometers) away. Great whites also use their eyesight, hearing, and **sensors** to quickly find food.

sensor – a small hole near a great white shark's mouth

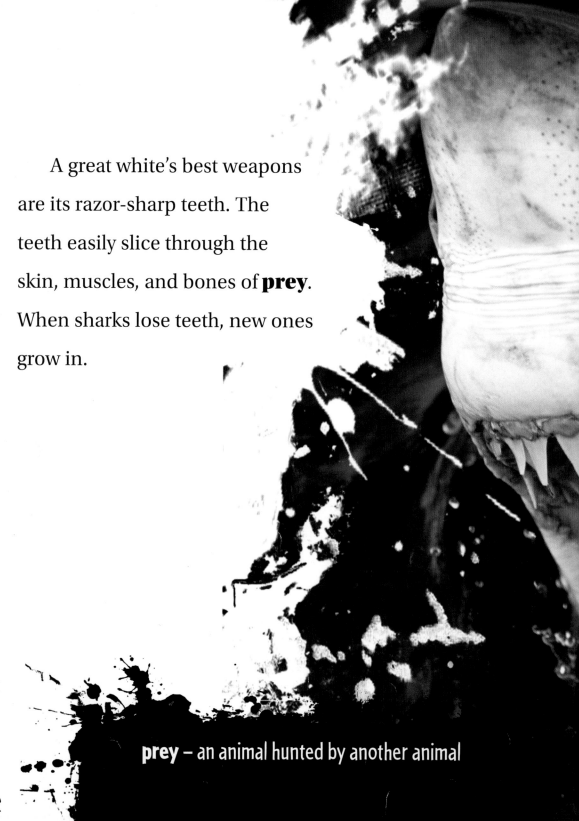

A great white's best weapons are its razor-sharp teeth. The teeth easily slice through the skin, muscles, and bones of **prey**. When sharks lose teeth, new ones grow in.

prey – an animal hunted by another animal

13

MAKING THE KILL

Great whites have gray backs.
Their backs help them blend in with
the ocean floor. Blending in helps
the shark sneak up on prey.

KILLER FACT

Great whites can jump as high as 6 feet (1.8 meters) out of the water.

KILLER FACT

Great whites mostly eat sea lions, seals, and sea turtles. They also eat dead animals.

A great white quickly kills its prey. It grabs prey with its jaws. The shark then shakes its head and tears off pieces of meat.

Sometimes a great white drops its prey after the first bite. The shark waits for the prey to bleed to death before eating it.

Great White Shark Diagram

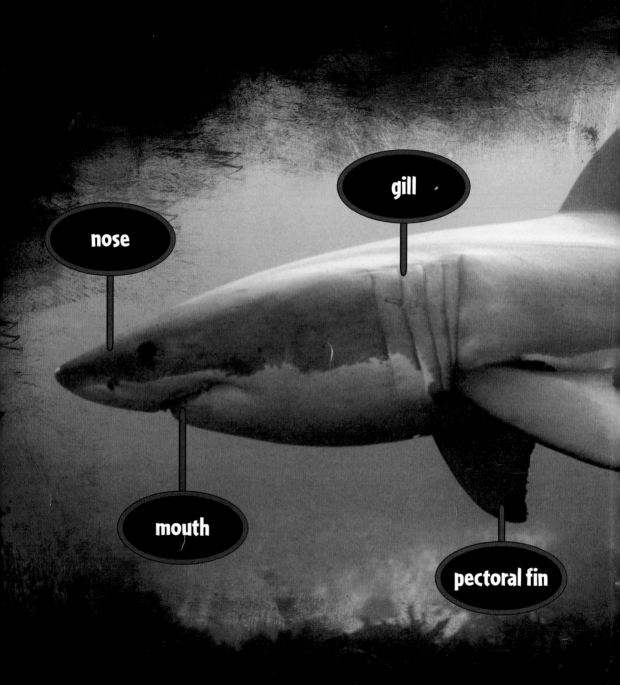

gill

nose

mouth

pectoral fin

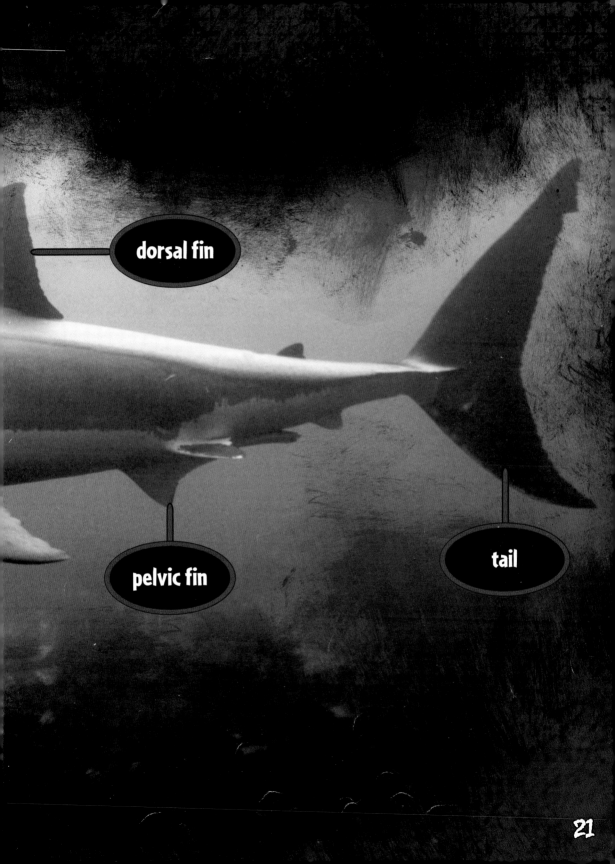

dorsal fin

pelvic fin

tail

HEADED FOR EXTINCTION?

Most people are afraid of great white sharks. But great whites don't attack people very often.

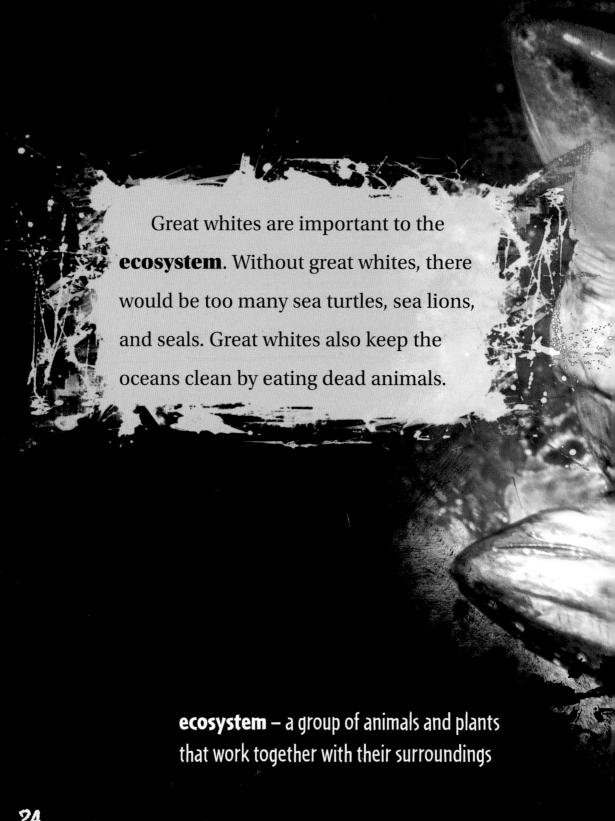

Great whites are important to the **ecosystem**. Without great whites, there would be too many sea turtles, sea lions, and seals. Great whites also keep the oceans clean by eating dead animals.

ecosystem – a group of animals and plants that work together with their surroundings

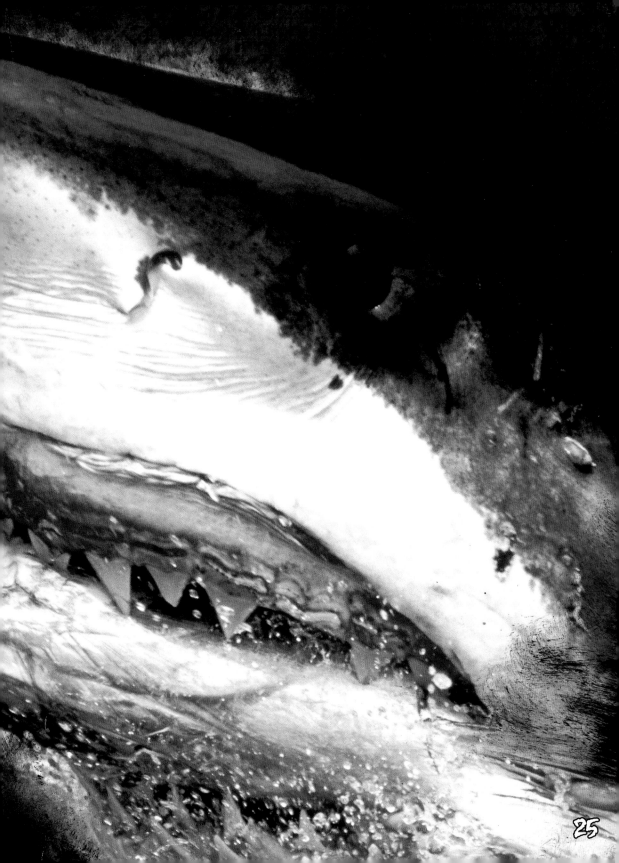

Fishing boats and hunters kill many great white sharks. Scientists are worried that great white sharks will become **extinct**. We must protect great whites so that they do not die out.

extinct – no longer living; an extinct animal is one that has died out, with no more of its kind.

Great Catch!

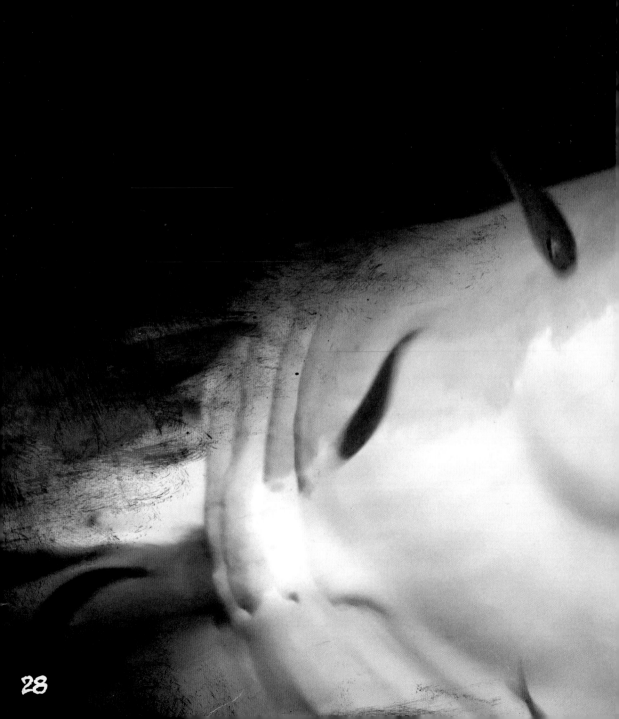

GLOSSARY

carnivore (KAHR-nuh-vohr) — an animal that eats only meat

ecosystem (EE-koh-sis-tuhm) — a group of animals and plants that work together with their surroundings

extinct (ik-STINGKT) — no longer living; an extinct animal is one that has died out, with no more of its kind.

prey (PRAY) — an animal hunted by another animal for food

seize (SEEZ) — to take something by force

sensor (SEN-ser) — a small hole near a great white shark's mouth

slice (SLISSE) — to cut through

READ MORE

Bredeson, Carmen. *Great White Sharks Up Close.* Zoom in on Animals! Berkeley Heights, N.J.: Enslow Elementary, 2006.

Simon, Seymour. *Sharks.* New York: Collins, 2006.

Thomas, Isabel. *Shark vs. Killer Whale.* Animals Head to Head. Chicago: Raintree, 2006.

INTERNET SITES

FactHound offers a safe, fun way to find educator-approved Internet sites related to this book.

Here's what you do:

1. Visit *www.facthound.com*
2. Choose your grade level.
3. Begin your search.

This book's ID number is 9781429623155.

FactHound will fetch the best sites for you!

INDEX